Metaverse Investing: A Guide for Beginners

Discover the Unending Opportunities and Risks of Investing in the
Digital Age

By Angela Lenns

Copyright

Table of Content

Introduction

In recent years, the term "metaverse" has gained widespread attention and has become a hot topic of discussion among tech enthusiasts, investors, and futurists. But what exactly is the metaverse, and why is it such a big deal?

The metaverse is a term used to describe a virtual world where users can interact with each other and digital objects in a three-dimensional space. It's essentially a fully immersive virtual reality experience that blurs the line between the physical and digital world. Think of it as a vast interconnected network of virtual worlds, games, and social platforms that allow users to experience new levels of social interaction, creativity, and entertainment.

As the metaverse continues to grow and evolve, it's becoming increasingly clear that it has the potential to revolutionize the way we live, work, and play. And as with any new and exciting technology, there are also ample opportunities for investment.

That's where this book, "Metaverse Investing: A Guide for Beginners" comes in. In this comprehensive guide, we will take a deep dive into the world of metaverse investing and explore the endless opportunities and risks associated with investing in this rapidly growing digital age.

Whether you're a seasoned investor looking to expand your portfolio or a curious beginner wanting to learn more about the metaverse, this book is the best plug. It will provide you with the tools and all the necessary information you need to invest wisely.

We'll start by breaking down the basics of the metaverse and explaining the key concepts that underpin this revolutionary technology. From there, we'll explore the various investment opportunities that the metaverse presents, including virtual real estate, digital currencies, and more.

With advancements in technology such as virtual reality, augmented reality, and blockchain, the metaverse is rapidly becoming a reality. Companies such as Facebook, Roblox, and Epic Games are investing billions of dollars into building out their metaverse platforms, and the potential for growth in this space is enormous.

Investing in the metaverse presents a unique opportunity for investors to get in on the ground floor of a rapidly evolving technology that has the potential to change the way we interact with the world around us. As virtual worlds become more sophisticated and captivating, they will become an increasingly important part of our daily lives. From virtual concerts and events to online shopping and education, the metaverse is set to transform a wide range of industries.

But with any investment opportunity comes risk, and the metaverse is no exception. One of the biggest risks associated with investing in the metaverse is regulatory uncertainty. As the metaverse becomes more mainstream, governments around the world are likely to step in and regulate the industry. This could have a significant impact on the value of investments in the metaverse, and investors need to be aware of these risks before diving in.

Another potential risk is the potential for market volatility. The metaverse is a rapidly evolving space, and there is still a lot of uncertainties around how the industry will develop in the coming years. This uncertainty could lead to fluctuations in the value of investments in the metaverse, and investors need to be prepared for these ups and downs.

Despite these risks, the potential rewards of investing in the metaverse are enormous. The metaverse is a technology that is set to transform our world in countless ways, and those who invest wisely in this space could see significant returns on their investment.

In "Metaverse Investing: A Guide for Beginners", we'll provide you with the knowledge and tools you need to make informed investment decisions in this exciting and rapidly evolving industry. Whether you're an experienced investor looking to diversify your portfolio or a newcomer to the world of investing, this book will provide you with the insights and advice you need to succeed in the metaverse. So join us on this exciting journey into the world of metaverse investing, and discover the unending opportunities and risks of investing in the digital age.

Chapter One:
What Is The Metaverse And What Makes It Worthwhile

The concept of the metaverse has been around for decades, popularized by science fiction novels and movies. However, it has recently gained momentum as a potential future of the internet. In short, the metaverse is a fully immersive virtual world. It's where users can interact with each other and digital objects in a seamless way. A manner similar to how we interact in the physical world. So, what does metaverse mean, and what's interesting about it?

At its core, the metaverse is a shared virtual space, where users can create their own avatars and interact with each other in real-time. It's not just a 3D video game or a social media platform, but a completely new type of digital experience. Metaverse is where users can explore, learn, create, and interact with the world in all new ways. The metaverse is not just a single platform or app, but a collection of interconnected virtual worlds, where users can travel between different environments seamlessly. It's just like we travel between cities or countries in the physical world.

The metaverse is often compared to the internet, but it's much more than that. While the internet is a collection of interconnected websites and services, the metaverse is a fully hypnotic 3D space, where users can experience things in a more natural and intuitive way. In the metaverse, you can attend virtual concerts, shop in virtual stores, take virtual classes, and even visit virtual versions of real-world locations. The possibilities are endless, and as the technology advances, the metaverse will become even more realistic and immersive.

So why should you care about the metaverse? Well, for one thing, it's likely to become a huge part of our digital lives in the near future. Just like how the internet has revolutionized the way we communicate and consume information, the metaverse has the potential to revolutionize the way we interact with each other and the world around us. It's not just a novelty or a gimmick, but a new way of experiencing and interacting with digital content.

The metaverse is also likely to create new opportunities for business, entertainment, education, and more. Already, companies like Roblox, Fortnite, and Minecraft have built virtual worlds that attract millions of users every day. As the technology improves, we can expect to see even more businesses and organizations building their own virtual spaces to connect with customers, partners, and fans.

In the metaverse, we can also expect to see new forms of social interaction emerge. Instead of scrolling through endless feeds and comments sections, users can interact with each other in a more natural and spontaneous way. They can attend virtual events together, collaborate on projects in real-time, and even build relationships that transcend the virtual world.

But like any new technology, the metaverse also raises important questions and concerns.

- Who will own and control the virtual spaces?

- Will it be accessible to everyone, or only to those who can afford the technology?

- Will it create new forms of inequality, or will it be a tool for social change?

These are all important questions that need to be addressed as we move towards a more metaverse-like future.

One of the most significant trends is the increasing sophistication of virtual and augmented reality technology. Over the past decade, companies like Oculus, HTC, and Microsoft have developed advanced headsets and software that can create highly immersive virtual environments. While these technologies are still relatively expensive and limited in their capabilities, they are rapidly improving, and it's likely that they will become much more accessible and affordable in the coming years.

Another important trend is the growth of online communities and social networks. Platforms like Facebook, Twitter, and Instagram have fundamentally changed the way we communicate and connect with each other, and the metaverse has the potential to take this to a whole new level. Instead of scrolling through a feed of photos and text, users can interact with each other in a more natural and responsive way, creating deeper connections and more meaningful experiences.

At the same time, there are concerns about the impact of the metaverse on privacy, security, and freedom of expression. With so much of our lives potentially taking place in virtual environments, it's important to ensure that users have control over their data and that their rights are protected. There are also concerns about the potential for virtual environments to be used for malicious purposes, such as cyberbullying or propaganda.

Although, the gains of the metaverse are so great, all that limitations notwithstanding. It has the potential to create new opportunities for entertainment, education, and commerce, as well as for social and political engagement. It could also help to break down barriers between people of different cultures and backgrounds, creating a more inclusive and interconnected world.

One important aspect of the metaverse is its potential to enable new forms of collaboration and creativity. In a virtual environment, people can work together on projects in real-time, regardless of their physical location. This could be particularly valuable for creative industries, such as gaming, film, and music, where collaboration is often key to success.

In the realm of education, the metaverse has the potential to create more engaging and interactive learning experiences. Students can explore virtual environments, interact with virtual objects, and collaborate with classmates in ways that are not possible in traditional classrooms. This could help to make education more accessible and inclusive, especially for students who live in remote or underprivileged areas.

In the realm of commerce, the metaverse could create new opportunities for businesses to connect with customers and partners in more captivating and interactive ways. For example, a company could create a virtual store where customers can browse products, interact with sales representatives, and make purchases in a seamless and engaging way. This could help to create more engaging and personalized shopping experiences, as well as to reduce the environmental impact of traditional retail.

Metaverse is an exciting and rapidly evolving concept that has the potential to fundamentally transform the way we interact with each other and the world around us. While there are still many questions and challenges to be addressed, it's clear that the metaverse is a future worth exploring and investing in. Whether you are a developer, a business owner, an educator, or simply a curious user, there are endless possibilities to be explored in this exciting new frontier.

In conclusion, the metaverse is a new and exciting concept that has the potential to change the way we interact with digital content and each other. It's not just a trend or a fad, but a new way of experiencing and engaging with the world around us. While there are still many questions and challenges to be addressed, the metaverse is a future worth exploring and investing in.

Chapter Two: Common Mistakes to Avoid When Investing in the Metaverse

The metaverse is the future of digital space and investment in this new world is rapidly growing. The possibilities are endless and the potential for profits is enormous. However, investing in the metaverse requires a unique set of skills and knowledge. In this chapter, we will explore the common mistakes to avoid when investing in the metaverse.

Mistake 1: Failing to Understand the Metaverse

One of the most common mistakes investors make when investing in the metaverse is failing to understand what it is. The metaverse is not just a new video game or virtual reality platform; it is a fully engaging digital world that combines elements of social interaction, entertainment, and commerce.

Investors who do not understand the metaverse and its potential are likely to make poor investment decisions. To avoid this mistake, it is essential to research and understand the basics of the metaverse, including its history, current state, and future potential.

Mistake 2: Investing in Unproven Projects

Investing in unproven projects is another common mistake that many investors make. With the rise of the metaverse, there has been an influx of new projects and startups that promise to revolutionize the digital world. However, many of these projects have not been thoroughly tested or proven to be successful.

Investors who invest in unproven projects are taking a significant risk with their money. Instead, it is essential to research the project thoroughly, understand its business model, and evaluate its potential for success before investing.

Mistake 3: Ignoring the Importance of User Experience

In the metaverse, user experience is everything. It is what makes the difference between a successful project and a failed one. Ignoring the importance of user experience is a common mistake that many investors make.

Investors who prioritize technology over user experience are likely to miss out on the potential of the metaverse. To avoid this mistake, it is essential to prioritize user experience and understand how it impacts the success of a project.

Mistake 4: Investing in Projects with Limited Utility

Investing in projects with limited utility is another common mistake that investors make. The metaverse has the potential to change many different industries, including gaming, entertainment, and e-commerce. However, some projects focus on a narrow range of applications or industries, limiting their potential for growth and profitability.

Investors who invest in projects with limited utility are likely to miss out on the potential of the metaverse. To avoid this mistake, it is essential to invest in projects that have a broad range of potential applications and industries.

Mistake 5: Failing to Diversify Investments

Diversifying investments is an essential strategy for any investor, and the metaverse is no exception. Failing to diversify investments is a common mistake that many investors make, putting all their money into a single project or platform.

Investors who fail to diversify their investments in the metaverse are taking a significant risk with their money. Instead, it is essential to invest in a range of projects and platforms, spreading out the risk and maximizing potential returns.

Mistake 6: Overlooking Regulation and Legal Issues

The metaverse is a new and rapidly evolving industry, which means that there are many regulatory and legal issues that need to be considered. Investors who overlook these issues are likely to run into problems down the road.

It is essential to understand the regulatory and legal landscape of the metaverse and how it impacts investments. This includes understanding issues such as data privacy, intellectual property, and cryptocurrency regulation.

Mistake 7: Focusing too much on Short-Term Gains

Investors who focus too much on short-term gains are likely to miss out on the long-term potential of the metaverse. The metaverse is still in its early stages, and it will take time for projects and platforms to mature and reach their full potential. Investors who focus only on short-term gains may sell their investments too early, missing out on future growth and profits.

To avoid this mistake, it is essential to have a long-term investment strategy that takes into account the potential for growth and profitability in the future.

Mistake 8: Underestimating the Importance of Community

The metaverse is built on the concept of community, and the success of any project or platform in the metaverse depends on its ability to build and maintain a strong community of users. Investors who underestimate the importance of community are likely to invest in projects or platforms that fail to gain traction and support.

To avoid this mistake, it is essential to evaluate the strength of a project's community and its ability to engage and retain users.

Mistake 9: Overlooking Technical Challenges

The metaverse is a complex and technically challenging environment, and projects. So platforms that fail to address these challenges are unlikely to succeed. Investors who overlook technical challenges are likely to invest in projects or platforms that suffer from technical issues or fail to deliver on their promises.

To avoid this mistake, it is essential to evaluate a project's technical capabilities and its ability to address the challenges of the metaverse.

Mistake 10: Neglecting to Stay Up-to-Date on Developments

The metaverse is a rapidly evolving environment, and new developments and innovations are happening all the time. Investors who neglect to stay up-to-date on these developments are likely to miss out on new opportunities or fail to recognize changes in the industry.

To avoid this mistake, it is essential to stay informed about developments in the metaverse and to adjust investment strategies accordingly.

In all, investing in the metaverse is a unique opportunity with the potential for significant profits. However, it also requires a specific set of skills and knowledge to navigate the complex environment of the metaverse. By avoiding common mistakes such as failing to understand the metaverse, investing in unproven projects, and neglecting to diversify investments, investors can maximize their potential for success in this new and exciting world.

Chapter Three:
Managing Your Emotions in Metaverse Investing: The Psychology of Risk and Reward

Investing in the metaverse, just like any other form of investment, can be a rollercoaster ride of emotions. One moment, you could be riding high on the euphoria of a big win, and the next, you could be consumed by the fear of a significant loss. This is why managing your emotions is critical in metaverse investing.

In this chapter, we will explore the psychology of risk and reward in metaverse investing, and how you can manage your emotions to make informed investment decisions.

The Psychology of Risk and Reward

The psychology of risk and reward is a fascinating subject, and it plays a significant role in metaverse investing. Understanding how it works can help you make better investment decisions and avoid emotional pitfalls.

The risk-reward ratio is the relationship between the potential reward of an investment and the amount of risk involved. For example, if an investment has a high potential reward, but it also has a high risk, the risk-reward ratio would be unfavorable. On the other hand, if an investment has a low risk but also a low potential reward, the risk-reward ratio would be favorable.

One of the most significant challenges of metaverse investing is assessing the risk-reward ratio. The metaverse is a relatively new and rapidly evolving field, and it can be challenging to assess the potential rewards accurately. Moreover, the risks associated with investing in the metaverse are high and varied.

Some of the risks associated with metaverse investing include technological risks, regulatory risks, and market risks. Technological risks arise from the complexity and newness of the technology underlying the metaverse. Regulatory risks arise from the uncertainty surrounding the legal framework for the metaverse. Market risks arise from the volatility of the metaverse market, which can be affected by many factors, such as changes in technology, new entrants, and economic conditions.

Managing Your Emotions

Investing in the metaverse can be an emotional rollercoaster. However, it would be best if you learned how to manage your emotions to make informed investment decisions.

The first step in managing your emotions is to recognize them. You need to be aware of how you are feeling about an investment and what is driving those feelings. This could be excitement, fear, greed, or something else entirely. Once you recognize your emotions, you can start to manage them.

One effective way to manage your emotions is to develop a set of investment criteria. This could include things like the risk-reward ratio, the quality of the team behind the investment, and the potential market size. By developing a set of investment criteria, you can make more informed investment decisions and avoid making impulsive decisions based on your emotions.

Another way to manage your emotions is to have a plan. This plan should include your investment goals, your risk tolerance, and your exit strategy. By having a plan, you can avoid making decisions based on your emotions and stick to your investment strategy.

In addition to developing a set of investment criteria, having a plan, and learning to control your emotions, there are several other strategies you can use to manage your emotions when investing in the metaverse.

One of these strategies is to stay informed. Keeping up to date with the latest news and developments in the metaverse can help you make more informed investment decisions and avoid reacting emotionally to short-term fluctuations in the market. You can follow industry news outlets, join online communities, and attend conferences and events to stay informed about the latest trends and developments in the metaverse.

Another strategy is to diversify your investments. Diversification is a critical strategy for managing risk in any investment portfolio. By investing in a diverse range of assets, you can reduce your exposure to any one asset or sector and minimize the impact of any one investment on your portfolio.

When investing in the metaverse, diversification could mean investing in a range of metaverse projects and companies, as well as other assets such as stocks, bonds, and cryptocurrencies. By diversifying your investments, you can also reduce the impact of any emotional reactions you may have to individual investments.

It is also important to stay patient when investing in the metaverse. The metaverse is a new and rapidly evolving field, and it may take some time before the potential rewards of your investments are realized. Therefore, it is important to have a long-term perspective when investing in the metaverse and to avoid making rash decisions based on short-term market fluctuations or emotional reactions.

When investing in the metaverse, it can be helpful to work with a financial advisor or investment professional. These are the people who understands the metaverse and can provide you with guidance and support. A good advisor can help you develop a sound investment strategy, manage your emotions, and navigate the complex and rapidly evolving metaverse market.

In conclusion, managing your emotions is critical when investing in the metaverse. By developing a set of investment criteria, having a plan, learning to control your emotions, staying informed, diversifying your investments, staying patient, and working with an advisor, you can make more informed investment decisions and avoid the emotional pitfalls that come with investing in this exciting but high-risk field.

Chapter Four:
Understanding Blockchain Technology and Its Role in the Metaverse

Blockchain technology has been making waves in various industries since its inception in 2008, with the creation of Bitcoin. In recent years, its potential applications have expanded beyond just cryptocurrency, and it has been touted as a game-changer in the realm of the Metaverse. In this chapter, we will dive into what blockchain technology is, how it works, and its potential applications in the Metaverse.

What is Blockchain Technology?

At its core, a blockchain is a decentralized digital ledger that records transactions in a secure and transparent manner. Instead of relying on a centralized authority or intermediary, such as a bank or government, transactions are validated and recorded by a network of nodes or computers that work together to maintain the integrity of the ledger. Each block in the chain contains a cryptographic hash of the previous block, creating a tamper-evident and immutable record of all transactions.

How Does Blockchain Technology Work?

Blockchain technology operates on a set of rules or protocols that define how nodes interact with each other and the blockchain. One of the key features of blockchain technology is its consensus mechanism, which ensures that all nodes agree on the state of the ledger. There are several consensus mechanisms, such as

Proof of Work (PoW) and Proof of Stake (PoS), that determine how nodes validate transactions and add new blocks to the chain.

In a PoW system, nodes compete to solve complex mathematical problems, and the first node to solve the problem is rewarded with newly minted coins or tokens. This process is known as mining and requires a significant amount of computational power and energy. PoS, on the other hand, relies on nodes staking or locking up a certain amount of coins or tokens to validate transactions and create new blocks. This method is considered more energy-efficient and environmentally friendly than PoW.

Potential Applications of Blockchain Technology in the Metaverse

The Metaverse refers to a virtual world or space that is inhabited by digital representations of people, objects, and services. It is a concept that has gained traction in recent years with the rise of virtual and augmented reality technologies. Blockchain technology has the potential to play a significant role in the Metaverse, particularly in the following areas:

Digital Identity
Blockchain technology can provide a secure and decentralized system for managing digital identities in the Metaverse. Users can have complete control over their identity and personal information, and third-party verification can be done in a transparent and tamper-evident manner.

Digital Assets

Blockchain technology can facilitate the creation and trading of digital assets in the Metaverse. These assets can include virtual real estate, digital art, in-game items, and even virtual currencies. Blockchain technology can ensure that these assets are unique, scarce, and verifiable, creating a thriving digital economy within the Metaverse.

Decentralized Governance

Blockchain technology can enable decentralized governance within the Metaverse, where decisions are made by a network of nodes or users rather than a centralized authority. This can help ensure that the Metaverse remains open and accessible to all, and that power is not concentrated in the hands of a few.

Transparency and Trust

Blockchain technology can increase transparency and trust within the Metaverse by providing a tamper-evident and immutable record of all transactions. Users can verify the ownership and history of digital assets, and the Metaverse can operate in a more transparent and accountable manner.

Interoperability

Blockchain technology can facilitate interoperability between different virtual worlds and platforms within the Metaverse. This can enable users to transfer digital assets and data seamlessly across different platforms, creating a more connected and integrated Metaverse.

facilitating a more open, secure, and accessible Metaverse, where users have greater control over their digital identity, assets, and interactions. By providing a tamper-evident and immutable record of transactions, blockchain technology can help build trust and foster a thriving digital economy within the Metaverse.

One of the key advantages of blockchain technology is its ability to create unique and scarce digital assets. In the Metaverse, these assets can take many forms, including virtual real estate, digital art, in-game items, and virtual currencies. By using blockchain technology, these assets can be created, tracked, and traded in a secure and transparent manner, creating a robust digital economy within the Metaverse. Furthermore, since blockchain-based assets are unique and verifiable, they can be used to represent real-world assets such as property or stocks, providing new opportunities for asset ownership and investment.

Another potential benefit of blockchain technology in the Metaverse is its ability to enable decentralized governance. In a decentralized governance system, decisions are made by a network of nodes or users rather than a centralized authority. This can help ensure that the Metaverse remains open and accessible to all, and that power is not concentrated in the hands of a few. Moreover, since blockchain technology provides a tamper-evident and transparent record of all transactions, it can help ensure that governance decisions are made in a fair and accountable manner.

Blockchain technology can also facilitate interoperability between different virtual worlds and platforms within the Metaverse.

Interoperability can enable users to transfer digital assets and data seamlessly across different platforms, creating a more connected and integrated Metaverse. This can help break down the silos that currently exist in the Metaverse and enable users to have a more unified and cohesive experience.

Moreover, blockchain technology can enhance the security and privacy of users in the Metaverse by providing a decentralized and tamper-evident system for managing digital identities. Users can have complete control over their identity and personal information, and third-party verification can be done in a transparent and verifiable manner. This can help reduce the risk of identity theft and fraud and provide users with greater peace of mind when interacting in the Metaverse.

In conclusion, blockchain technology has the potential to play a significant role in the development of the Metaverse. By enabling secure and transparent transactions, creating unique and scarce digital assets, facilitating decentralized governance, promoting interoperability, and enhancing security and privacy, blockchain technology can help create a more open, connected, and accessible Metaverse. However, as with any new technology, there are also challenges and risks that must be addressed, including scalability, energy consumption, regulatory uncertainty, and the potential for market manipulation. Nonetheless, the potential benefits of blockchain technology in the Metaverse are significant. It is likely that we will see continued innovation and experimentation in this space in the years to come.

Chapter Five:
Opportunities in the Metaverse: Gaming, NFTs, Virtual Real Estate, and More

This chapter explores the various opportunities that exist within the metaverse, which is the collective virtual space created by the convergence of augmented reality, virtual reality, and the internet. It highlights some of the key areas of the metaverse, such as gaming, NFTs, and virtual real estate, and discusses the potential opportunities and challenges that come with each.

Gaming is one of the most popular activities in the metaverse, and it has been a significant driver of growth for the industry. In-game purchases and virtual goods sales have become a significant source of revenue for game developers, and this trend is expected to continue. One of the major opportunities in gaming is the ability to create immersive and engaging experiences that can keep players coming back for more. Game developers can leverage the latest technologies such as virtual reality and augmented reality to create more immersive and interactive games.

The use of non-fungible tokens (NFTs) has also opened up new opportunities for creators and developers within the metaverse. NFTs are unique digital assets that can be bought, sold, and traded on blockchain platforms. They can represent anything from virtual real estate to virtual items within a game. The use of NFTs has created new revenue streams for creators and developers, who can earn royalties from the sale of their digital assets. NFTs have also opened up new opportunities for artists and musicians, who can use them to sell digital art and music.

Another significant opportunity within the metaverse is virtual real estate. Virtual real estate is similar to physical real estate in that it can be bought, sold, and developed. However, virtual real estate exists within the metaverse and can be used to create virtual experiences, such as shopping malls, amusement parks, and even virtual cities. Virtual real estate can also be used as a platform for advertising and marketing, creating new opportunities for businesses to reach consumers.

One of the main challenges with virtual real estate is creating a sense of scarcity and exclusivity. Since virtual real estate is unlimited, there is no inherent scarcity, which can make it difficult to create a sense of value. However, developers can create scarcity by limiting the amount of virtual real estate available or by creating exclusive virtual communities.

In addition to gaming, NFTs, and virtual real estate, the metaverse offers numerous other opportunities for businesses and entrepreneurs. For example, virtual events, such as conferences and concerts, have become increasingly popular within the metaverse. Virtual events can be more accessible and inclusive than physical events, as they can be attended from anywhere in the world.

Virtual education is another area of the metaverse that is experiencing significant growth. Online learning has become increasingly popular in recent years, and the metaverse offers a more immersive and interactive way of learning. Virtual classrooms and educational simulations can help students learn in a more engaging and memorable way.

However, there are also several challenges associated with the metaverse. One of the main challenges is the issue of interoperability. The metaverse is made up of multiple virtual worlds and platforms, each with its own rules and standards. This can make it difficult for users to move between different platforms and for developers to create applications that work across multiple platforms.

Another challenge is the issue of privacy and security. The metaverse is a digital space, and as such, it is susceptible to hacking and other security breaches. Users also need to be aware of the privacy implications of using virtual spaces, such as the collection of personal data by virtual world operators.

Privacy and security are also critical challenges that need to be addressed to ensure the safety and protection of users in the metaverse. As virtual spaces become more integrated into our daily lives, it is important to ensure that user data is protected and that virtual world operators adhere to privacy regulations. The use of blockchain technology and decentralized systems can provide a more secure and transparent way of managing user data and transactions in the metaverse.

Another challenge that needs to be addressed is the issue of accessibility. While the metaverse offers new opportunities for businesses and entrepreneurs, it is important to ensure that everyone has equal access to these opportunities. This includes addressing issues such as the digital divide and ensuring that virtual spaces are accessible to people with disabilities.

It is important to consider the ethical implications of the metaverse. As virtual spaces become more integrated into our daily lives, it is important to ensure that they are designed and operated in an ethical and responsible manner. This includes addressing issues such as virtual addiction, cyberbullying, and the impact of virtual experiences on mental health.

Despite these challenges, the metaverse offers a vast array of opportunities for businesses and entrepreneurs. As virtual experiences become more immersive and interactive, the metaverse has the potential to revolutionize industries such as gaming, entertainment, education, and even real estate. By leveraging the latest technologies and addressing the challenges associated with the metaverse, businesses and entrepreneurs can create new and exciting experiences that transform the way we live, work, and play.

Finally, the metaverse offers numerous opportunities for businesses and entrepreneurs in areas such as gaming, NFTs, virtual real estate, virtual events, and education. However, there are also several challenges that need to be addressed in order to fully realize the potential of the metaverse.

Interoperability is a key challenge that needs to be addressed. This is because it can limit the growth of the metaverse and hinder the development of new applications and experiences.

Interoperability standards, such as the Open Metaverse Interoperability Protocol (OMIP), can help address this challenge by enabling the creation of a shared virtual space where different virtual worlds and platforms can connect and interact.

Chapter Six: Assessing Potential Risks and Rewards of Metaverse Investments

Investing in the metaverse can be both exciting and risky. While there is the potential for significant returns, there are also numerous uncertainties and challenges to consider. Therefore, it is crucial to evaluate the potential risks and rewards of metaverse investments before diving in. In this chapter, we will discuss some of the key factors to consider when assessing the potential risks and rewards of metaverse investments.

Technological Risks
Metaverse investments are inherently tied to technology, and as such, there are several technological risks to consider. These risks may include:

Security risks: The metaverse is built on a complex network of interconnected systems, making it vulnerable to security breaches. A single hack can cause significant damage to the entire network, affecting all investments.

Compatibility risks: The metaverse is still in its early stages, with different platforms using different technologies. This lack of standardization can make it difficult for investors to navigate and ensure compatibility between different platforms.

Scaling risks: The metaverse is expected to experience significant growth in the coming years. However, if the infrastructure is not designed to handle this growth, it could result in performance issues and reduced functionality.

Legal and Regulatory Risks: Metaverse investments are subject to legal and regulatory risks, which can vary significantly by jurisdiction. Some of the legal and regulatory risks to consider may include:

- **Unclear legal status**: The legal status of the metaverse is still evolving, with many questions surrounding ownership, intellectual property, and liability. These uncertainties can create significant risks for investors.

- **Regulatory challenges:** As the metaverse grows in popularity, regulators may begin to scrutinize its activities more closely. Investors may face regulatory challenges that could impact the value of their investments.

- **Jurisdictional risks:** The metaverse operates across multiple jurisdictions, each with its own laws and regulations. Investors may face challenges navigating these legal complexities, especially if they are investing in multiple jurisdictions.

Financial Risks

Metaverse investments are subject to the same financial risks as any other investment. These risks may include:

- **Market risks:** The value of metaverse investments can be highly volatile, especially in the early stages. Investors may experience significant fluctuations in value, which can result in significant gains or losses.

- **Liquidity risks:** Metaverse investments may be illiquid, meaning that investors may not be able to sell their investments quickly or at fair market value.

Counterparty risks: Metaverse investments often involve multiple parties, such as developers, platform owners, and other investors. These parties may have varying degrees of reliability and solvency, which can impact the value of investments.

Technical Risks
Technical risks refer to risks that arise from the technical implementation of metaverse investments. These risks may include:

- **Incomplete or inadequate implementation:** Metaverse projects are complex and require a significant amount of technical expertise. If the implementation is incomplete or inadequate, it can result in functional issues and reduced value for investors.

- **Difficulty in integration:** The metaverse is a complex ecosystem, and integrating new technologies or applications can be challenging. If integration is not successful, it can result in reduced value for investors.

- **Maintenance risks:** Metaverse projects require ongoing maintenance and updates. If maintenance is not performed properly, it can result in functional issues and reduced value for investors.

Social Risks: The metaverse is a social space, and as such, it is subject to social risks. These risks may include:

- **Reputational risks:** Metaverse projects are subject to public scrutiny, and negative publicity can impact the value of investments. Investors should be aware of reputational risks associated with the projects they are investing in.

- **User adoption risks**: The success of metaverse projects is dependent on user. If users did not get value for their money, they are bound to abandon the system. This could spell doom for the exciting technology like this.

Chapter Seven:
Implementation of Diversification Strategies in Metaverse Portfolios

In the previous chapters, we have discussed various diversification strategies that can be implemented in a metaverse portfolio. In this chapter, we will delve into the practical implementation of these strategies.

Diversification is a fundamental principle of portfolio management, and it is equally important in the metaverse as it is in the real world. A well-diversified portfolio can provide investors with exposure to multiple assets, thereby reducing their overall risk. The implementation of diversification strategies involves selecting a mix of assets with varying degrees of risk and return potential, and combining them in a way that balances the risks and rewards.

One of the most effective ways to diversify a metaverse portfolio is to invest in a range of different metaverse assets, such as virtual real estate, gaming assets, digital art, and cryptocurrencies. Each of these asset classes has its own unique characteristics and risks, and a diversified portfolio can help mitigate the risks associated with any one asset class.

Another approach to diversification in the metaverse is to invest in different metaverse platforms. There are several metaverse platforms available, each with its own unique set of features and applications. By investing in a range of platforms, investors can reduce their exposure to the risks associated with any one platform.

A key aspect of implementing a diversification strategy in the metaverse is portfolio rebalancing. Portfolio rebalancing involves periodically adjusting the portfolio's holdings to maintain the desired level of diversification. This may involve selling assets that have become overvalued and reinvesting the proceeds in undervalued assets, or adjusting the portfolio's allocation to different asset classes or platforms.

In addition to diversifying across asset classes and platforms, investors can also diversify within each asset class or platform. For example, within the virtual real estate asset class, investors can diversify by investing in properties in different metaverse platforms, or by investing in properties with different features or locations.

Another way to diversify within a metaverse portfolio is to invest in assets with different liquidity profiles. Some metaverse assets, such as cryptocurrencies, are highly liquid and can be easily bought and sold on exchanges. Others, such as virtual real estate, may be less liquid and require more time and effort to sell.

Investors should also consider the tax implications of their diversification strategy. Depending on the jurisdiction, the tax treatment of different metaverse assets may vary. Investors should consult with a tax professional to determine the best strategy for their specific situation.

The implementation of a diversification strategy requires a disciplined approach, and it is essential to regularly review and rebalance the portfolio to maintain the desired level of diversification. This can be done by setting a target allocation for each asset class or platform and periodically rebalancing the portfolio to ensure that it remains aligned with the target allocation.

For example, suppose an investor has a target allocation of 40% in virtual real estate, 30% in gaming assets, 20% in cryptocurrencies, and 10% in digital art. If the value of the virtual real estate holdings increases over time, the portfolio may become overweight in this asset class. In this scenario, the investor may choose to sell some of their virtual real estate holdings and reinvest the proceeds in the other asset classes to rebalance the portfolio.

Diversification strategies can be applied to both passive and active investment approaches. Passive investment approaches, such as index funds or ETFs, can provide broad exposure to a range of asset classes and platforms. Active investment approaches, on the other hand, involve selecting individual assets and platforms based on research and analysis. Active investors can use diversification strategies to manage risk and increase the potential for long-term returns.

The metaverse is a rapidly evolving landscape, and the diversification strategies that are effective today may not be effective in the future. It is essential for investors to stay informed about new developments and trends in the metaverse and adjust their portfolios accordingly.

One potential risk associated with diversification strategies in the metaverse is the concentration of power among a small number of dominant platforms. For example, if one platform becomes overwhelmingly dominant, it may be challenging for investors to diversify their portfolios effectively. In this scenario, investors may need to adjust their diversification strategies to focus on niche platforms or asset classes.

Another potential risk associated with diversification in the metaverse is the lack of regulation and oversight. The metaverse is still largely unregulated, and investors may be exposed to fraud or other forms of misconduct. Investors should conduct thorough due diligence and research before investing in any metaverse asset or platform.

So, investors should be mindful of the risks associated with diversification. While diversification can reduce overall risk, it cannot eliminate it entirely. Investors should carefully evaluate the risks associated with each asset class and platform, and diversify their portfolio accordingly.

To cap it up on this topic, implementing a diversification strategy in a metaverse portfolio requires careful consideration of a range of factors. The factors includes: asset class, platform, liquidity, and tax implications. A well-diversified portfolio can provide investors with exposure to multiple assets, thereby reducing their overall risk.

Chapter Eight:
Regulatory and Legal Considerations for Investing in the Metaverse

As the metaverse continues to expand and mature, regulatory and legal considerations become increasingly important for investors. In this chapter, we will discuss some of the key areas that investors should be aware of when investing in the metaverse, including regulatory frameworks, legal risks, and compliance requirements.

Regulatory Frameworks
The metaverse is a global phenomenon that operates across borders and jurisdictions, which means that navigating regulatory frameworks can be complex. Governments around the world are still grappling with how to regulate the metaverse, and different countries have taken different approaches.

In the United States, for example, the Securities and Exchange Commission (SEC) has been closely monitoring the development of virtual assets and has issued guidance on how existing security laws may apply to certain types of digital assets. Other countries, such as China, have taken a more restrictive approach, banning certain activities related to virtual assets altogether.

Investors should be aware of the regulatory environment in the countries where they are investing and should seek legal advice if they are uncertain about the legal status of a particular virtual asset or transaction.

In addition to the regulatory frameworks in different countries, investors should also be aware of the different regulatory bodies and laws that may apply to virtual assets. For example, in the United States, the SEC has been particularly active in monitoring the virtual asset space and has taken enforcement action against companies that violate securities laws.

Investors should also be aware of the potential for regulatory changes as the metaverse continues to evolve. As virtual assets become more popular and mainstream, it is likely that governments will continue to take a more active role in regulating the space.

Legal Risks

In addition to regulatory risks, investors in the metaverse face a number of legal risks. And the greatest limitation of this technology is it's vunerability to cyber crime. Because the metaverse is largely unregulated, it is easier for bad actors to create fake virtual assets or to engage in other fraudulent activities.

Investors should be wary of any investment opportunity that seems too good to be true, and should carefully research any virtual assets or platforms before investing. They should also be aware of the risks associated with storing virtual assets in wallets or on exchanges, as these platforms are often targeted by hackers.

Another legal risk for investors in the metaverse is the potential for intellectual property disputes. As the metaverse grows, it is likely that disputes over ownership of virtual assets or intellectual property rights will become more common. Investors should be aware of the risks associated with investing in virtual assets that may be subject to these types of disputes.

One legal risk that investors should be particularly aware of is the risk of money laundering and other illicit activities. Because the metaverse is largely anonymous and decentralized, it is easier for criminals to use virtual assets for illegal purposes.

Investors should be aware of the potential for virtual assets to be used in money laundering, terrorist financing, and other criminal activities, and should take steps to ensure that their investments are not being used for these purposes.

Investors should also be aware of the potential for legal disputes between users of virtual assets. For example, if two users claim ownership of the same virtual asset, it may be difficult to resolve the dispute without the involvement of legal authorities.

Compliance Requirements

Finally, investors in the metaverse should be aware of the compliance requirements that apply to virtual assets. Depending on the jurisdiction and the type of virtual asset, investors may be subject to a range of regulatory requirements, including registration, reporting, and disclosure obligations.

Investors should also be aware of the tax implications of investing in virtual assets. In many jurisdictions, virtual assets are subject to capital gains tax, and investors may be required to report their virtual asset holdings to tax authorities.

One compliance requirement that is particularly important for investors in the metaverse is know-your-customer (KYC) and anti-money laundering (AML) requirements. Many virtual asset platforms and exchanges are required to collect and verify user information in order to comply with these regulations.

Investors should also be aware of the potential for tax implications when investing in virtual assets. Depending on the jurisdiction, virtual assets may be subject to capital gains tax or other taxes, and investors may be required to report their holdings to tax authorities.

Therefore, investors should be aware of the potential for changes to compliance requirements as the regulatory landscape continues to evolve. It is possible that new regulations or compliance requirements may be introduced in the future. This could impact the way that investors are able to invest in virtual assets.

Investing in the metaverse can be exciting and lucrative, but it is important for investors to be aware of the regulatory and legal risks involved. By understanding the regulatory environment, researching virtual assets and platforms before investing, and being aware of compliance requirements, investors can minimize their risk and make winning investment decisions.

Chapter Nine:
Understanding the Importance of Intellectual Property Rights in the Metaverse

The metaverse is a digital realm that is constantly evolving and expanding. As the metaverse grows, it becomes increasingly important for investors to consider the implications of intellectual property (IP) rights in this new frontier. This chapter will explore the significance of IP rights in the metaverse, why they matter for investors, and what steps they can take to protect their investments.

The Importance of Intellectual Property Rights

Intellectual property refers to the legal ownership of creative works, such as music, art, and writing. In the metaverse, IP rights are especially important because of the potential for user-generated content (UGC) to become a major source of revenue. UGC refers to content created by users, such as avatars, clothing, and virtual environments. Investors who own IP rights to UGC can potentially earn royalties from the sale of those items in the metaverse.

Additionally, IP rights protect investors from the unauthorized use of their content. Without IP protection, anyone could copy and distribute UGC without compensating the original creator. This could result in a loss of revenue for investors and discourage future investment in the metaverse.

Types of Intellectual Property Rights

There are several types of intellectual property rights that investors should be aware of in the metaverse. They are:

Copyrights: Copyrights protect original works of authorship, such as music, art, and writing. In the metaverse, copyrights can protect UGC created by users.

Trademarks: Trademarks protect brand names and logos. In the metaverse, trademarks can be used to protect the identity of virtual businesses and products.

Patents: Patents protect inventions and processes. In the metaverse, patents can protect new technologies and virtual products.

Trade Secrets: Trade secrets protect confidential information, such as formulas, designs, and business strategies. In the metaverse, trade secrets can be used to protect proprietary algorithms and software.

Limitations To Intellectual Property Right in the Metaverse

The metaverse presents several challenges to the protection of intellectual property rights. One major challenge is the difficulty in enforcing IP rights across different virtual worlds and platforms. Because the metaverse is decentralized, there is no central authority to regulate IP infringement. Additionally, because virtual items can be easily replicated and distributed, it can be challenging to prove ownership of UGC.

Another challenge is the potential for IP theft through hacking and other malicious activities. Investors must take steps to protect their IP from cyber threats and ensure that their UGC is secure.

Protecting Intellectual Property Rights in the Metaverse
Despite these challenges, investors can take steps to protect their intellectual property rights in the metaverse. Some strategies include:

Registering IP: Investors should register their IP with the relevant authorities to establish legal ownership and make it easier to enforce their rights.

Using Digital Watermarks: Digital watermarks can be used to identify and track UGC, making it easier to prove ownership and detect unauthorized use.

Employing Security Measures: Investors should use security measures such as encryption, firewalls, and two-factor authentication to protect their IP from cyber threats.

Participating in Metaverse Governance: Investors should participate in metaverse governance to help establish rules and regulations for the protection of IP rights.

As the metaverse continues to grow, intellectual property rights will become increasingly important for investors. By understanding the different types of IP, the challenges to protecting them, and the strategies for safeguarding their investments, investors can position themselves for success in this exciting new frontier.

Beyond protecting their own intellectual property, investors should also consider the broader implications of IP rights in the metaverse. One important consideration is the impact of IP on innovation and creativity in the virtual world.

On one hand, strong IP protections can encourage investment in the development of new technologies and content. When creators know that they can profit from their work, they are more likely to invest time and resources in innovation. This can lead to a more vibrant and diverse metaverse ecosystem, with a wider variety of content and experiences for users.

On the other hand, overly restrictive IP protections can stifle innovation and creativity. When creators are limited in their ability to build on and remix existing content, they may be less likely to experiment with new ideas. This could lead to a less dynamic and diverse metaverse, with fewer opportunities for users to explore and create.

As investors consider the role of IP in the metaverse, they should aim to strike a balance between protecting their investments and fostering innovation and creativity. This may involve supporting initiatives that promote fair use and open access to content, as well as advocating for policies that balance the interests of content creators and consumers.

Another important consideration for investors is the potential for IP conflicts and disputes in the metaverse. With so many creators and users interacting in a single virtual space, there is a high likelihood of overlap and duplication of content. This can lead to disputes over ownership and infringement, which can be difficult to resolve in a decentralized environment.

To mitigate these risks, investors should be proactive in their approach to IP management. This may involve working with legal and regulatory experts to establish clear guidelines and policies for IP ownership and use. It may also involve participating in metaverse governance initiatives to help shape the development of IP standards and best practices.

In conclusion, intellectual property rights are a critical consideration for investors in the metaverse. By understanding the different types of IP, the challenges to protecting them, and the broader implications of IP in the virtual world, investors can position themselves for success in this exciting new frontier. As the metaverse continues to evolve, it will be essential for investors to remain vigilant and proactive in their approach to IP management, in order to protect their investments and promote innovation and creativity in the virtual world.

Chapter Ten:
NFTs and Metaverse Gaming In 2023

The gaming industry has long been one of the most significant and lucrative sectors in the entertainment industry, and the rise of the metaverse is only making it more prominent. As virtual worlds become more complex and immersive, the line between gaming and the metaverse begins to blur. In this chapter, we will explore how Non-Fungible Tokens (NFTs) are transforming the gaming industry in the metaverse and how they are becoming a new investment trend to watch in 2023.

NFTs and Gaming in the Metaverse

NFTs are special kind of digital money kept on the blockchain. They can be anything from a piece of art to a tweet, a GIF, or even an in-game item. One of the most significant advantages of NFTs is that they allow for ownership and transferability of virtual assets in a way that was not possible before.

In the metaverse, NFTs are revolutionizing the gaming industry by allowing players to own and trade virtual assets such as weapons, skins, and even entire virtual worlds. For example, in Decentraland, a virtual world built on the Ethereum blockchain, players can buy and sell virtual land using NFTs. This means that virtual land can be owned and developed just like real-world land, creating a new opportunity for investment in the metaverse.

NFTs are also changing the way gamers interact with the games they play. Instead of being limited to in-game purchases, players can now buy and sell assets outside of the game. This creates a new secondary market for virtual assets, which is already worth millions of dollars. It is expected to grow even further as more gamers enter the metaverse.

Investing in NFTs in the Metaverse

Investing in NFTs in the metaverse can be a profitable venture for those who are willing to take the risk. However, it is important to do your research before investing in any virtual asset. Here are some of the ways you can invest in NFTs in the metaverse:

Buying and Selling NFTs: Just like any other asset, NFTs can be bought and sold on various marketplaces. Some of the popular NFT marketplaces include OpenSea, Rarible, and SuperRare. The value of an NFT depends on various factors such as rarity, popularity, and demand.

Investing in Gaming Companies: As the gaming industry continues to grow in the metaverse, investing in gaming companies can be a profitable investment. Look for companies that are developing games for the metaverse or those that are integrating NFTs into their games.

Investing in Virtual Real Estate: As mentioned earlier, virtual real estate is becoming a popular investment opportunity in the metaverse. You can buy virtual land and develop it to create unique experiences for other players. Companies like Somnium Space and The Sandbox are leading the way in this space.

NFTs are transforming the gaming industry in the metaverse and are becoming a new investment trend to watch in 2023. As the metaverse continues to evolve, we can expect to see more opportunities for investment in virtual assets. However, it is important to approach any investment in the metaverse with caution and do your research before making any decisions.

Certainly! In recent years, NFTs have gained significant attention in the art world, but they are now making their way into the gaming industry. NFTs are becoming increasingly prevalent in metaverse gaming, allowing gamers to own and trade in-game assets with the potential for real-world value. This trend is expected to grow in 2023, making NFTs and metaverse gaming an exciting new investment opportunity.

One of the key advantages of NFTs in gaming is the ability to offer players true ownership of in-game assets. Traditionally, gamers have only been able to buy virtual items that have no real-world value and cannot be traded or sold outside of the game. NFTs, on the other hand, can be bought, sold, and traded on various marketplaces, allowing gamers to truly own their virtual assets. This is a significant change that is already transforming the gaming industry, and it is expected to continue to do so in the coming years.

Another key benefit of NFTs in gaming is the potential for new revenue streams. Traditionally, gaming companies have relied on in-game purchases to generate revenue. With NFTs, however, gaming companies can create a new revenue stream by allowing players to own and trade virtual assets. This not only benefits the gaming companies but also the gamers who can potentially make a profit by buying and selling in-game assets.

One of the most exciting aspects of NFTs and metaverse gaming is the potential for investment opportunities. In addition to buying and selling NFTs on marketplaces, investors can also invest in gaming companies that are developing games for the metaverse or those that are integrating NFTs into their games. As the metaverse continues to grow, investing in virtual real estate is also becoming a popular investment opportunity. Investors can buy virtual land and develop it to create unique experiences for other players.

While the potential for investment opportunities in NFTs and metaverse gaming is significant, it is important to approach any investment with caution. As with any new industry, there is always a level of risk involved. It is crucial to do thorough research and seek the advice of experienced investors before making any investment decisions.

In conclusion, NFTs and metaverse gaming are an exciting new investment trend to watch in 2023. As virtual worlds become more complex and engaging, the potential for NFTs in gaming is expected to grow. This presents new opportunities for both gamers and investors, but it is important to approach any investment with caution and to do thorough research before making any decisions.

Chapter Eleven:
Implementing Your Winning Metaverse Investment Strategy

Congratulations! You've made it this far, and you now have a solid understanding of the metaverse and how it may transform our lives in the years to come. In the previous chapters, we've explored the various aspects of building a winning metaverse investment strategy, including identifying the right investment opportunities, evaluating the risks and rewards of each option, and determining your risk tolerance and investment goals.

In this chapter, we'll discuss how to put your winning metaverse investment strategy into action. Below are few of vital steps necessary:

Evaluate your portfolio
Before making any investment decisions: it's important to evaluate your current portfolio. Determine what percentage of your investments are allocated to the metaverse, and how those investments are performing. If you have a significant percentage of your portfolio in the metaverse, you may want to consider diversifying your holdings to reduce risk.

Identify the right investment opportunities:
Now that you've evaluated your portfolio, it's time to identify the right investment opportunities. Consider the various sectors within the metaverse, such as gaming, social media, virtual reality, and e-commerce. Look for companies that are leaders in their

respective sectors, have a solid track record of growth and profitability, and have a clear vision for the future.

Determine your investment strategy:
There are several investment strategies you can use when investing in the metaverse, including long-term buy and hold, dollar-cost averaging, and swing trading. Consider your investment goals and risk tolerance when .determining which strategy is right for you.

Execute your investment plan:
Once you've determined your investment strategy, it's time to execute your plan. This may involve opening new investment accounts, purchasing shares of specific companies or exchange-traded funds (ETFs), and monitoring your investments regularly. Be sure to stay up-to-date on the latest news and developments within the metaverse industry, as this can impact your investment decisions.

Re-evaluate and adjust as necessary:
Finally, it's important to re-evaluate your investment strategy regularly and adjust as necessary. This may involve rebalancing your portfolio, reallocating your investments based on performance, or adjusting your investment goals. Remember that investing in the metaverse is a long-term strategy, and it's important to stay focused on your goals and adjust your strategy as needed.

Sure! Let's dive a bit deeper into each step of implementing your winning metaverse investment strategy.

Step 1: Evaluate Your Portfolio

Before making any investment decisions, it's important to evaluate your current portfolio. This includes not only your investments in the metaverse but also your investments in other sectors. Look at the overall allocation of your investments and determine if you are overexposed to any one area. For example, if you have a large percentage of your portfolio invested in tech stocks, you may want to consider diversifying into other sectors, such as healthcare or consumer goods.

When evaluating your metaverse investments specifically, consider how those investments have performed over time. Have you seen consistent growth and profitability, or have there been periods of volatility and decline? Evaluate each investment on its own merits and consider whether it aligns with your long-term investment goals.

Step 2: Identify the Right Investment Opportunities

Once you've evaluated your portfolio, it's time to identify the right investment opportunities within the metaverse. Start by considering the various sectors within the metaverse, such as gaming, social media, virtual reality, and e-commerce. Look for companies that are leaders in their respective sectors, have a solid track record of growth and profitability, and have a clear vision for the future.

When evaluating individual companies, consider factors such as their financial performance, market share, and competitive advantages. Look for companies with strong management teams and a clear strategy for growth. It's also important to consider the overall market trends within the metaverse and how those trends may impact specific companies and sectors.

Step 3: Determine Your Investment Strategy

There are several investment strategies you can use when investing in the metaverse, including long-term buy and hold, dollar-cost averaging, and swing trading. Consider your investment goals and risk tolerance when determining which strategy is right for you.

A long-term buy and hold strategy involves purchasing shares of a company with the intention of holding onto those shares for a period of years. This strategy can be beneficial for investors who are willing to be patient and ride out short-term fluctuations in the market.

Dollar-cost averaging involves investing a fixed amount of money at regular intervals, regardless of market conditions. This strategy can be beneficial for investors who want to reduce the impact of market volatility on their portfolio.

Swing trading involves buying and selling stocks based on short-term market fluctuations. This strategy can be beneficial for investors who are comfortable taking on more risk in exchange for the potential for higher returns.

Step 4: Execute Your Investment Plan

Once you've determined your investment strategy, it's time to execute your plan. This may involve opening new investment accounts, purchasing shares of specific companies or ETFs, and monitoring your investments regularly. Be sure to stay up-to-date on the latest news and developments within the metaverse industry, as this can impact your investment decisions.

One way to stay informed is by following industry publications and news outlets, such as Forbes, TechCrunch, and VentureBeat. You can also attend industry conferences and events, such as the Virtual Worlds Best Practices in Education Conference or the Virtual Reality Developers Conference.

Step 5: Re-evaluate and Adjust as Necessary

Finally, it's important to re-evaluate your investment strategy regularly and adjust as necessary. This may involve rebalancing your portfolio, reallocating your investments based on performance, or adjusting your investment goals. Remember that investing in the metaverse is a long-term strategy, and it's important to stay focused on your goals and adjust your strategy as needed.

In conclusion, investing in the metaverse can be a lucrative opportunity for long-term investors, but it requires careful planning, research, and execution. By following the steps outlined in this chapter, you can create a solid investment plan that aligns with your goals and risk tolerance.

Chapter 12:
Balancing Traditional Investments with Metaverse Investment

Investing in the metaverse may seem like a new and exciting opportunity. However, it's important to remember that traditional investments still have a place in a balanced portfolio. In this chapter, we'll explore how to balance traditional investments with metaverse investment and why it's important to do so.

The Importance of Diversification

Diversification is the key to a well-balanced portfolio. It's a risk management technique that involves investing in a variety of different assets to reduce the overall risk of the portfolio. By spreading your investments across different asset classes, you can potentially minimize the impact of any one investment's poor performance.

The same principle applies to balancing traditional investments with metaverse investment. While the metaverse may offer exciting opportunities, it's important not to put all your eggs in one basket. By diversifying your investments, you can reduce the overall risk of your portfolio and potentially achieve better long-term returns.

Understanding Risk and Return

When it comes to investing, risk and return go hand in hand. In general, higher-risk investments have the potential to generate higher returns, while lower-risk investments typically offer lower returns. It's important to find the right balance between risk and return that suits your investment goals and risk tolerance.

When balancing traditional investments with metaverse investment, it's important to consider the risk and return profiles of each investment. Traditional investments like stocks and bonds are generally considered lower-risk investments, while investments in the metaverse, such as NFTs or virtual real estate, may be higher-risk investments. As such, it's important to understand the potential risks and returns of each investment and allocate your investment capital accordingly.

Finding the Right Allocation

Finding the right allocation between traditional investments and metaverse investments will depend on your individual investment goals and risk tolerance. In general, younger investors with a higher risk tolerance may be more willing to allocate a larger portion of their portfolio to metaverse investments. On the other hand, more conservative investors may prefer to stick to more traditional investments and allocate only a small portion of their portfolio to the metaverse.

Ultimately, the right allocation will depend on a number of factors, including your investment goals, risk tolerance, and investment time horizon. It's important to work with a financial advisor to determine the right allocation for your individual needs and circumstances.

Monitoring Your Portfolio

Once you've found the right allocation between traditional investments and metaverse investments, it's important to monitor your portfolio regularly to ensure that it remains in balance. As market conditions and individual investments change over time, your portfolio may become unbalanced, requiring you to rebalance your portfolio by buying or selling certain investments.

Monitoring your portfolio can help you stay on track towards your investment goals and adjust your investments as needed. This will help to keep your portfolio balanced and aligned with your investment strategy.

One important consideration when balancing traditional investments with metaverse investment is the potential for correlation between different investments. Correlation refers to the degree to which two investments move in tandem with one another. When two investments are highly correlated, they tend to move in the same direction at the same time. This can increase the overall risk of a portfolio if one or more investments experience a downturn.

It's important to consider correlation when allocating investments between traditional assets and metaverse assets. For example, if you already have a significant allocation to technology stocks in your traditional portfolio, you may want to limit your allocation to metaverse investments, as there may be a high correlation between technology stocks and certain metaverse assets.

Another important factor to consider when balancing traditional investments with metaverse investment is liquidity. Traditional investments like stocks and bonds are generally highly liquid, meaning that they can be bought and sold quickly and easily without significantly affecting their market price. In contrast, some metaverse assets, such as virtual real estate, may be less liquid and may take longer to sell.

When allocating investments to the metaverse, it's important to consider the liquidity of each investment and the potential impact of a lack of liquidity on your portfolio. This may mean limiting your allocation to less liquid metaverse assets or diversifying your metaverse investments across a range of different asset classes.

It's also important to consider the potential for regulatory risk when investing in the metaverse. The metaverse is a relatively new and rapidly evolving space, and regulations around metaverse investments are still being developed. As such, it's important to stay up-to-date on regulatory developments and potential risks when allocating investments to the metaverse.

Investing in the metaverse can be an exciting opportunity, but it's important to remember that traditional investments still have a place in a well-balanced portfolio. By diversifying your investments and finding the right allocation between traditional investments and metaverse investments, you can potentially reduce risk and achieve better long-term returns.

Remember to work with a financial advisor to determine the right allocation for your individual needs and circumstances and to monitor your portfolio regularly to ensure that it remains balanced and aligned with your investment goals. With the right approach, you can balance traditional investments with metaverse investments and potentially achieve your investment goals while taking advantage of the exciting opportunities offered by the metaverse.

Overall, balancing traditional investments with metaverse investment requires careful consideration of a range of factors, including correlation, liquidity, and regulatory risk. Working with a financial advisor can help you navigate these complexities and develop a well-balanced investment strategy that aligns with your individual goals and risk tolerance.

Conclusion

In conclusion, "Metaverse Investing: A Guide for Beginners" is a comprehensive and informative book that has introduced the exciting world of metaverse investing. As the metaverse continues to gain popularity and evolve, it is essential for beginners to understand the opportunities and risks involved in investing in this market.

Through this book, you have learned the basics of metaverse investing, including what the metaverse is, how it works, and why it has the potential to revolutionize the way we live, work, and play. You have also gained insight into the various investment options available in the metaverse, such as cryptocurrencies, virtual real estate, and non-fungible tokens (NFTs).

It is important to remember that investing in the metaverse, like any other investment, requires careful consideration and due diligence. The market is still in its early stages, and while the potential for growth is significant, there are also risks and uncertainties involved. However, with the knowledge and tools provided in this guide, you are better equipped to make informed investment decisions in the metaverse.

As you embark on your metaverse investing journey, always remember to stay informed, stay curious, and stay vigilant. With the right mindset and approach, you can navigate this exciting and dynamic market and potentially reap the rewards of metaverse investing.